Sea Glass Secrets

Julia Reesor

Sea Glass Secrets

ISBN: 9798399100357

Sea Glass Secrets

For Liam,

You saved me from the sea.

Sea Glass Secrets

Contents

Shatter

Sea glass begins as shattered pieces,
swallowed by the sea.

Sea Glass Secrets

The waves whispered secrets.
The shores stored answers.

The beach.

The home of many, yet only meaningful to one.

The hurt.

Discarded remnants of once beautiful treasures laid delicately along the shore, a humble gift from the waves to the hurt.

All buried,
except for one.

Its opaque light blue colour caught my eye.

Glass.

I picked it up and delicately turned it over in my hand,
admiring its smooth texture and sharp edges.

A prism of light, reflecting the early morning sun's glow.
Reflecting beauty for all to see.

I was captivated.

The shard of glass slipped from my fingers,
slicing me as it dropped into the sand's warmth.

I was hurt.

The Shatter.

Sea Glass Secrets

The first memory I ever have is of boxes.

Boxes littering the dark, narrow hallway
once filled with light.

Boxes stacked higher than I am in a room
that echoes the distant memory of laughter.

Boxes stealing memories from each room it resides in,
locking them up forever.

My life belonged in boxes.

Peculiar men with ironed uniforms walk in and out of
my room with my memories in their hands.

Memories my father and I made.
Memories my mother and father made.
Memories my brother and I made.
Memories that no longer belong in this house.

I wonder if the next family will care for my mother's hydrangeas
that she planted in the front yard on my third birthday.

I wonder if the next family will coat the pink walls of
my bedroom with a different colour.

I wonder if the next family will consist of a mother and father
who love each other.

I wonder, where I'm going.

Sea Glass Secrets

I watch the waves from the ocean I now call home,
tickle my bare toes before it retreats.

I bury my toes into the warm sand,
wondering what critters live beneath the surface.

I stretch my arms up over my head,
grasping for the afternoon sun that only wants to hurt me.

I wonder if my father lives near the ocean like I do now.
I wonder if my father buries his toes into the warm sand.
I wonder if my father grasps for the afternoon sun.

I wonder, where he is.

Sea Glass Secrets

I was told he would teach me to ride a bike.
I don't know how to ride a bike.

I was told he would take me to my favourite amusement park.
I have never been to my favourite amusement park.

I was told he would scare away the monsters under my bed.
The monsters still live under my bed.

I was told to call him Dad.
I don't know what a Dad is.

Sea Glass Secrets

I yearned for a mother I saw in movies.
I yearned for a mother I saw my friends had.
I yearned for a mother I read about in books.

One where their love was unconditional.
One where their adoration was given effortlessly.
One where their light guided you on your darkest days.

The love she gave me was conditional.
The adoration she gave me was exhausting to give.
The light she gave me was dimmed.

She was my Mom.
Yet she never made me feel like she was.

Sea Glass Secrets

His regular path through the backyard
is starting to dent the grass with his footprints.

His voice is echoed throughout
the walls of my house late at night.

I smell his cologne when
I sit on the couch in the morning.

His vague essence mirrors the ghosts that
loom the darkened hallways as my siblings and I sleep.

We know he is there, but we can never prove it.

From my memory, he is tall.
He has dark brown hair and wears glasses.
He likes to wear sweaters.
Knitted sweaters.

My mother wears knitted sweaters now.

Sea Glass Secrets

Distant memories of a lost love
now belong in shattered pieces.

The pieces are buried.
The memories are abandoned.
The love is lost.

I am the reminder of a lost love.

The distance between my mother and I grew.
She filled the void with someone new.

The distance between my father and I grew.
He filled the void with someone new.

I am the reminder of the void that only grew.

I watched them grow their new lives on alternate weekends.
I watched them grow their new lives on separate holidays.

As I watched them build new pieces.
As I watched them make new memories.
As I watched them find new love.

I was reminded.

Of a love that was lost.
Of a love that left me in the growing void.

Sea Glass Secrets

I stood on the beach's shore,
rooted in place.

The waves tickled my toes,
before retreating into the unknown.

With every ebb and flow,
they stole with it the footprints that once stood next to me.

The footprints of my family.
The footprints of my friends.

Scattering them to sea,
and away from me.

And yet here I stood.

On the beach's shore,
rooted in place.

Sea Glass Secrets

The outside of my house is perfect.

The outer walls are painted in a bright yellow colour.
The plants that circle its perimeter are lush with life and vibrancy.
The roof is sloped, yet stable.
The atmosphere it encompasses is beautiful.

The inside of my house is damaged.

The inner walls are painted white
and hide secrets beneath their chipped paint.

The staircase creaks in the right places
to alert those either below or above.

The dining room table is suitable for eight
but never seats one.

The stained-glass window features a crack
from an object that was not meant to hit it.

The atmosphere it encompasses is suffocating with secrets.

Outer eyes see its perfection.
Inner eyes see its destruction.

Sea Glass Secrets

Your favourite drink is clear.
It has a pungent smell.
It flows in unison as it circles the melting ice cubes in your glass.

From your lips.
To your throat.
To your stomach.
To your head.
To your words.
To your fists.

That is the path the clear liquid takes every night.

When you drink it, it makes you powerful.
When you drink it, it makes you angry.

When you drink it, it makes you forget.

When you drink it, it makes me weak.
When you drink it, it makes me empty.

When you drink it, I never forget.

Sea Glass Secrets

The last time I felt my mother's love
was when I was in her womb.

She spent nine months delicately curating me.

My eyes.
My heart.

When she laid her eyes on me for the first time,
she realized she could never love me.

My eyes saw through her.
My heart followed a different beat.

She discarded me the day she laid her eyes on me.

I was made with love.
I was not made to be loved.

Sea Glass Secrets

You had scars from your mother.
Burrowed under your skin.
Neglect passed down to you.

I have scars from my mother.
Burrowed under my skin.
Neglect passed down to me.

My daughter will not have scars from her mother.
They will not be burrowed under her skin.
Neglect will not be passed down to her.

I will break the cycle.

Sea Glass Secrets

My brother looks just like our father.
Anytime I miss our father, I look at him.

I look just like our mother.
Anytime I look in the mirror, I look away.

Sea Glass Secrets

I am sick of being sick.

The shallow rocks I used to navigate with ease,
now trip me as I walk.

The fog I used to dance through with ease,
now cloud my mind as I think.

The sun I used to grasp for with ease,
now burns me as I reach.

I wish I could explain this life sentence
I was burdened with when my life started.

A life sentence of being hurt from the shallow rocks.
A life sentence of being clouded by the fog.
A life sentence of being burned by the sun.

A life sentence of being sick.

Sea Glass Secrets

My issues with my father started with my mother.

Hushed conversations around open ears.
Sorrowful sobs watched by young eyes.
Poisonous words cracking the heart of a child.

I no longer hear my father the same.
I no longer see my father the same.
I no longer love my father the same.

I hear my father with the same ears my mother does.
I see my father with the same eyes my mother does.
I love my father with the same heart my mother does.

Sea Glass Secrets

My stability was echoes from strange voices
in the middle of the night.

Comforting you.

My stability was clear liquids
in the middle of the day.

Comforting you.

My stability was echoes.
My stability was liquids.

Stealing the comfort you were
supposed to provide me.

Sea Glass Secrets

The bus ride home from school made me painfully aware
that I was going to a house.

A house where there is no light seen during the day.
A house where the nights are too dark for comfort.
A house where laughter has never echoed off the walls.
A house where hushed conversations involve all.
A house where love is never willingly given.

A house I am forced to call home,
yet has never felt like one.

Sea Glass Secrets

I leave my secrets buried in the four walls
of a home I only knew as a house.

Where they are not seen by outer eyes.

Four walls that my friends will never see.
Four walls that my teachers will never see.

My secrets gifted me with a mask to wear
when I leave the four walls.

I wear it with my friends.
I wear it with my teachers.

My mask disappears when I return to the
home I only know as a house.

My secrets leave their burrow in the walls.

Where they are seen by my eyes.

Sea Glass Secrets

My home has a heart.
My home has lungs.
My home has a brain.
My home has 206 bones.

My home heals me when my heart breaks.
My home heals me when my chest feels tight.
My home heals me when my brain works against me.
My home heals me when I physically break.

My home doesn't have my love.

Sea Glass Secrets

When I spoke,
you held a mirror in front of my face.

When I cried,
you bought yourself tissues for your tears.

My voice was muffled.
Your voice was clear.

My sobs were hushed.
Your sobs were deafening.

I will hear your voice until I take my last breath.

It was the only voice I heard in the depths of the night.
In the wake of my sorrows.

Your voice.
Your hurt.

Always yours,
never mine.

Sea Glass Secrets

I didn't have the emotional or physical
connection of any parent.

I was stranger to love.
I was stranger to communication.

I was starved of hugs.
I was starved of their presence.

I grew to learn that love is transactional.
I grew to learn that communication is a flaw.
I grew to learn that hugs are uncomfortable.

I grew to learn that their absence carved a void
I would be craving until I take my last breath.

Sea Glass Secrets

By the time I was sixteen,
I had seen three different sets of divorce papers.

Each were written with passion and anger.
Each were abandoned with contentment and hope.

The first one collected dust on our coffee table.
The second one collected dust on our dining room table.
The third one collection dust on our kitchen island.

The ink never stained the paper.
The meaning stained my heart.

Their inkless signature was a reminder of their power.
Their power over me.

Sea Glass Secrets

I am torn between anger and empathy.

The nights when you abandoned me,
I was angry for feeling your neglect.

Yet I understood you wanted to feel loved.

The days when you closed the door to parenting,
I was angry for feeling your distance.

Yet I understood you never had a parent.

I am angry because I wanted to feel loved.
I am angry because I wanted to have a parent.

Yet I understand I was too hard to love.
Yet I understand I was too much of a burden.

Sea Glass Secrets

I threw a lifeline to someone I loved.

In the time I had known them,
I felt as though I truly knew them.

In the time they had known me,
I felt as though they never truly knew me.

They wanted to be a lawyer.
I wanted to be loved.

They wanted four kids.
I wanted to be a kid.

As time progressed,
I realized that they had never caught my lifeline.

They let the line I threw float beside them,
and instead gave me a wooden raft.

One that was flimsy.
One that was cracked.
One that cut me and gave me splinters.

One that eventually sank,
swallowing me with it.

Sea Glass Secrets

Sleepless nights fostered a mind of wonders.

Wondering if it was my touch.
My tone.
My heart.
My soul.

That made you walk away without so much
as a lingering glance.

And yet throughout all of the wonders,
I would end up empty handed.

Wondering why your touch felt so fleeting.
Wondering why your tone felt so cold.
Wondering why your heart felt so distant.
Wondering why your soul felt so detached from mine.

And yet throughout all of the wonders,
I would end up empty handed.

Without an apology.
Without an excuse.

Without my hands full of the closure I deserve.

Sea Glass Secrets

Your infidelity didn't break me.

It made me insecure.
It made me hesitant.
It made me guarded.
It made me sorrowful.

It made me many things.
But it didn't break me.

You can't break something that is already broken.

Sea Glass Secrets

When the hit stained my cheek,
I stood rooted in place.

When the poisonous words branded my heart,
I stood rooted in place.

When the neglect burrowed deep into my spirit,
I stood rooted in place.

When the war was against me,
I stood rooted in place.

When I left,
I kept the door open a crack.

A pre-emptive measure for when I return.
I knew I would return.

Return to the stained cheeks.
Return to the poisonous words.
Return to the neglect.
Return to the war.

Return to the family that never made me feel loved.

Sea Glass Secrets

I was born without a voice.
I let my older sibling speak for me.

I was born without an identity.
I let my younger sibling find one for me.

I chose to spend my days on a fence,
harbouring between being in the shadow or overlooked.

The shadow made me feel cold.
Being overlooked made me feel desolate.

The fence made me feel safe.

Safe from the voice that was not mine.
Safe from the identity that was not mine.

Safe from the reminder that I was born in the middle.

Sea Glass Secrets

The moment I was born, I shattered.
My delicate pieces were swallowed by the sea.

Shattered by expectations out of my grasp.
Shattered by empty seats at dinner tables.
Shattered by watching doors open and close without me.

The turbulent waters washed what was left of my shattered
being along the beach, for all to admire and cherish.

They would admire.
They would cherish.

They would walk away.

I am sea glass.

Forever left on the beach.
Admired and cherished, then walked away from
without a second thought.

I am the youngest child.

Forever left behind.
Admired and cherished, then walked away from
without a second thought.

Sea Glass Secrets

My biggest secret is the broken house
I know as a home.

My biggest secret is the destruction
that lies within it.

I don't let the suffocating secrets slip out of the cracks.

I keep them buried.
I am prepared to keep them buried for the rest of my life.

My friends think I am busy on the weekends.
My teachers think I got lazy with my assignments.

My siblings think I am their parent.

I think I am a kid.

Sea Glass Secrets

I sacrificed Saturday nights out with my friends,
for staying in and reading you a book before bed.

Without my sacrifice,
your books would collect dust beside your bed.

I sacrificed going on dates with new faces,
for making you dinner at home.

Without my sacrifice,
your dinner would remain uncooked.

I sacrificed being a child,
to care for you as a child.

Without my sacrifice,
your childhood would become shattered like mine.

Sea Glass Secrets

I hated being called mature for my age.
I didn't ask to be mature.

It was forced upon me like a prophecy.

It made me disconnect from friendships because
I didn't have the same aspirations as them anymore.

It made me wish for a different life because
I didn't have the energy for the life I had anymore.

It made me grow up faster than I needed to.

It made me mature.
It made me lonely.

Sea Glass Secrets

I was the friend born into a broken home.

The chains that bound me to the brokenness
gave me enough space to travel to other homes.

Ones where I saw love.
Ones where I saw compassion.
Ones where I saw empathy.

I would grasp at the love.
I would embrace the compassion.
I would cradle the empathy.

Holding onto as much of it as I could,
before my chains pulled me back into the brokenness.

Where I saw sorrow.
Where I saw animosity.
Where I saw distance.

Where I saw what I only knew.
Brokenness.

Sea Glass Secrets

Watching my friends be loved by their parents
made me resentful.

I resented their effortless laughter.
I resented their easy communication.
I resented their unconditional adoration.

It made me insecure.
It made me sorrowful.
It made me confused.

How could love be granted so easily,
yet has never touched the steps of my home?

Sea Glass Secrets

My heart begged to be held.

Held by someone with warm hands.
Held by someone with a soft touch.

My hands were too cold to cure its broken pieces.
My hands were too scarred to cure its shattered being.

I had seen others being held
by their parents during heartbreak.

I always wondered if that was the secret.

A parent's warm hands used to glue the pieces.
A parent's soft touch used to cure the shattering.

I handed my heart to my parents.

And it shattered twice.

Once from heartbreak.
Once from the courage I had to ask them for kindness.

Sea Glass Secrets

I tried to find the silence in sobriety.
I tried to find the light in sobriety.

For my friends, who cried at my state.
For my family, who cried for the person I once was.

I found its noise was too piercing.
I found its light was too clear.

I slipped back into the shadows.

Where the noise was muffled.
Where the light was dim.

The feelings were muffled.
The guilt was dim.

In the shadows, I am my own enemy.
In the shadows, I am my own saviour.

Destroying myself.
Restoring myself.

An endless cycle I wish to end.
An endless cycle I am too comfortable with to end.

Sea Glass Secrets

The hurt consumed me.
It chewed at parts of my heart that still felt.

Decaying it.
Breaking it.
Bruising it.

Each time the hurt became unbearable,
I unwrapped a bandage.

Placed it over the hurt.
Squeezed it once for good measure.

And tried again.

When I placed my fragile heart in your hands,
you gave it back to me.

With fresh hurt.
With worn bandages.

And yet I still reached for a new bandage.
And yet I still tried again.

Sea Glass Secrets

I felt my heartstrings break for the first time when I was twelve.
I mended them back together.

With delicate hands, and a reassuring embrace.

I felt them break again when I was fourteen.
I mended them back together.

With delicate hands, and an open ear.

I felt them break again when I was seventeen.
I mended them back together.

With delicate hands, and a comfortable moment of silence.

I felt them break again when I was twenty.
I mended them back together.

With delicate hands,
a reassuring embrace,
an open ear,
and a comfortable moment of silence.

I only ever had myself.

Sea Glass Secrets

I always believed I took up space.
Too much space.

The feeling that I was too much,
suffocated me.

I took up space in every friendship.
I took up space in every relationship.
I took up space in every connection.

I took up space to make up for
the space I didn't have in my own home.

Sea Glass Secrets

You told me that mother-daughter
relationships were bound by complexity.

Your rendition of complexity
danced to the tune of hatred.

Your rendition of complexity
danced to the tune of anger.

Your rendition of complexity
danced to the tune of bitterness.

Your rendition of complexity
danced to the tune of neglect.

I begged for it to dance to a different tune.

Sea Glass Secrets

I believe I was born into a broken home.
Born into it like a destiny.

Where shrieking sounds were normal.
They comforted you in the darkness.

Where foreign objects thrown at innocent walls were normal.
They filled the deafening silence.

Where redness branding your cheeks were normal.
They made you feel something other than pain.

A destiny where I only knew a broken home to be home.

Sea Glass Secrets

I have a blind spot.
It grows more each day.

It grows to envelop my vision,
blurring all it touches.

It grows to claim my control,
making me a spectator to my former self.

I dream of a world without a blind spot.

A world with clear vision.
A world with control.

Yet clear vision can't exist.
Yet control can't exist.

With me in it.

A world without a blind spot would be one without me in it.

Sea Glass Secrets

When the nights were filled with harrowing screams,
I held you until you fell asleep.

When I was going to sleep, I held myself.

When the days were filled with neglect,
I held you until you felt loved.

When I felt neglected, I held myself.

When the feelings of anger were pointed towards me,
I shielded you from the war.

When the anger hit me, I shielded myself from the war.

When your tears stained your pillow,
I let you sleep with mine.

When my tears stained my pillow,
I let the dampness soften my sobs.

When I attempted to fly,
you let your sadness seep from the shadows.

I watched your tears fall.
I watched my feet remain rooted in place.

Ready to stay who I was born to be.

A bird with clipped wings.

Sea Glass Secrets

My wings were clipped.
Chaining me to the house that has never been a home.

Your wings were dented.
Trying to chain you to the house that has never been a home.

I used to soar.
Now I watch you soar.

Away from the house
that has never been a home.

Clipped wings make others soar.

Sea Glass Secrets

A burning house provided me with stability.

I knew which side of the roof would cave in first.
I knew which window would crack first.

I knew every deafening scream in the darkened night.
I knew every ghost that loomed the hallways.

I knew you were the match that lit the house.

The house I was forced to call home.

Sea Glass Secrets

My body felt itchy.

Thousands of ants crawling across my skin,
marking it with the reminder that I would rather be
anywhere else than here.

They tickled my mind.

Feeding it with thoughts of loathing.
Feeding it with feelings of hate.
Feeding it with moments of comparison.

The only time when I felt relief from their
constant swarm was when I itched.

I hated itching.
But I hated myself more.

Sea Glass Secrets

When they asked about my mother,
I told them she was not around much.

Only I knew that she was searching for
love in anyone but her children.

When they asked about my siblings,
I told them they were doing well.

Only I knew that my arms were
the only ones that held them during their darkest nights.

When they asked about my father,
I told them he was away for the night.

Only I knew his absence stretched
beyond the nights.

They always questioned.
My lies always answered.

Sea Glass Secrets

In the moments where I needed light,
I knew not to turn to you.

In the moments where I needed support,
I knew not to lean on you.

In the moments where I needed love,
I knew not to expect it from you.

You taught me where not to turn to.
You taught me where not to lean on.
You taught me where not to expect from.

I knew none about where I could turn to.
I knew none about where I could lean on.
I knew none about where I could expect from.

Sea Glass Secrets

I counted fourteen days on the calendar in our kitchen.

Two trips to the grocery store.
Two loads of laundry.
Fourteen walks with the dogs.
Nine times the sun woke me up.
Four rainy days stuck in a house that was not a home.

I crossed off the fourteenth day on the calendar,
and went upstairs to read my siblings a book before bed.

Where are you?

Sea Glass Secrets

11:57pm.
I looked at the tree in the corner of the room.
My gifts to my siblings were the only ones placed under it.

11:58pm.
I looked at the kitchen.
Empty pizza boxes littered the counters from dinner.

11:59pm.
I looked at the living room.
My siblings and I were the only ones who occupied it.

12:00am.
I looked over at my siblings.
A feather from one of their wings had fallen.

Holidays are visible reminders of abandonment.

Sea Glass Secrets

My mother found her purpose in others.

I wish my mother found her purpose
in being a mother.

Sea Glass Secrets

Hushed murmurs from outside voices
told me I needed to forgive.

They were told a piece of the story,
and decided for me that forgiveness was the antidote.

The piece they were told didn't capture
the harrowing screams in the depths of the night.

The piece they were told didn't capture
the days painted with abandonment.

The piece they were told didn't capture
the unjustifiable hurt inflicted on a child.

And yet they sat there,
with the piece in their hands.

Handing me forgiveness.

What if I don't want to forgive?

Sea Glass Secrets

The door had been open my entire life.

I often dreamed about what I would see on the other side.

Would I see destruction?
Would I see red cheeks?

I dreamed, yet never left.

I let the cool breeze of the door's openness
tempt me into creating the life I wish they created for us.

I was tempted, yet never left.

Until the destruction became too destructive.
Until the red cheeks became too red.

And I walked out into the unknown.

You said you were happy to see me finally free.

I broke my own heart leaving you chained.

I will come back for you.

Sea Glass Secrets

On my birthday,
I turned tired.

Tired from spending years being an adult.

Years when my mother
decided to stop being a mother.

Years when my father
decided to stop being a father.

Years when my siblings
had no choice but to look to me as their parent.

Tired from spending my childhood being an adult.

Sea Glass Secrets

I became well acquainted with a bottle
when I was twelve years old.

It danced in the darkened hallways of my house.
It suffocated me in the depths of the night.
It stained the lips of my parents.

Its damage was all I grew to know.

As I grew older, it made me resent growing up.

I felt out of place at dinner parties.
I felt insecure on Saturday nights.
I felt isolated from my friends during nights out.

A bottle broke me as a child.
I now feel broken as an adult.

Sea Glass Secrets

From paragraphs to sentences.
The texts went dry.
From sleepovers to silence.
The void only grew.

We spent every waking moment together.

Laughing.
Crying.
Sharing secrets.

Your mother said I was her second child.
I felt at home when I walked into your home.

Until it shifted.

We no longer laughed.
We no longer cried.
We no longer shared secrets.

You no longer knew me.

I stopped being the first to reach out.
I figured that was what you wanted.
Less of me.

When I stopped reaching out, I got less of you.
Less and less, until there was none.

A friendship ended with distance.
Our friendship ended with distance.

Sea Glass Secrets

I haven't seen the friends I said I would love forever,
in forever.

We crossed the stage.
We danced our last dance.
We cried in each other's arms.

And then we dispersed into the crowd.

The text messages went cold.
The daily updates became yearly.
The constant check-ins became inconstant.

The crowd became thick.

Thick with new stages.
Thick with new dances.
Thick with new arms.

Sea Glass Secrets

I grew comfortable with broken promises.

I grew comfortable with their
lasting scars on my skin.

I grew comfortable with their
shattering hurt on my heart.

I grew comfortable with their
echoes of empty words in my ears.

I grew comfortable enough with them
that I let them break me.

Now, a broken promise is just a promise.

Sea Glass Secrets

I gathered my courage.

Delicately holding years of hurt
in my fragile hands.

I dusted off the neglect.
I scrapped off the pain.
I washed off the tears.

I handed it to you.
You handed it back to me.

The apology loose on your lips
never reaching your voice.

Never reaching my ears.
Never reaching my heart.

Sea Glass Secrets

My name flows from your lips.

Coated in illusion.
Dripping in deception.

Dancing into the ears of your friends.

You tell them how I'm doing.
You tell them pieces of my life I haven't told you.
You tell them you will say hello the next time you see me.

You don't tell them that we haven't spoken in two years.

Sorrow

Sea glass dances in the ocean's sorrows.

Sea Glass Secrets

The waves whispered secrets.
The shores stored answers.

The beach.

The home of many, yet only meaningful to one.

The sorrowful.

Discarded remnants of once beautiful treasures laid delicately along the shore, a humble gift from the waves to the sorrowful.

All buried,
except for one.

Its opaque light blue colour made its mark amongst the sand's warmth.

The glass that hurt me.

I picked it up and delicately turned it over in my hand,
admiring its smooth texture and sharp edges.

A prism of light, reflecting the afternoon sun's glow.
Reflecting beauty for all to see.

I was captivated.

The shard of glass graced my fingers,
before it landed in the ocean's lapping waves.

I was sorrowful.

The Sorrow.

Sea Glass Secrets

The words from your diagnosis rang in my ears.
The picture on the scan pulled at my heart.

The words were muffled by the sound of my heart.
The picture was silenced by the sound of my heart.

Not from the sound of it racing.
Not from the sound of it beating.

From the sound of my heartstrings breaking.

Sea Glass Secrets

56 bright lights lit up the scan.

They twinkled against the grey and white image.

In every artery.
In every bone.
In every organ.

In any place that required oxygen.
In any place that once felt something other than pain.

Their glow was too bright for me to see.
I shielded my eyes.
I looked away.

Their meaning was too clear for me to see.
I shielded my eyes.
I looked away.

They tell you that cancer is a disease.

But what they don't tell you is that
it can shatter a human heart in two.

Sea Glass Secrets

You wear hats inside the house
because your head gets cold.

You wear extra-large knitted sweaters
to provide your body with additional warmth.

You went down six pant sizes
yet won't acknowledge that you did.

You are becoming more forgetful after each treatment.

I knitted you a hat.
I wash your extra-large knitted sweaters.
I bought you new pants.

I remind you of my name.

Sea Glass Secrets

The hospital walls are made of straw.

Four walls that once provided me with hope,
have become undone.

There was nothing left for me at the hospital anymore.
No reason for me to sit in the uncomfortable leather chair.
No reason for me to return.

When I walked out of the hospital the day you died,
I believe I never truly left.

The person I was when I walked in,
and the person I was when I walked out,
are now different.

One was filled with hope.
One is filled with grief.

The part of me clinging to the hope that you will
walk out with me is still there.

I think it will always be there.

Sea Glass Secrets

When you took your last breath,
I forgot how to breathe.

When you closed your eyes for the last time,
my vision became clouded.

When your voice was no longer heard,
I forgot how to speak.

When you died,
a piece of me died that day too.

Sea Glass Secrets

The day your soul left this earth,
was the day mine did too.

My heart no longer beats the same.
My eyes no longer see the same.
My mind no longer thinks the same.

While I am physically here,
my soul is with yours.

Bound together in the stars.

Sea Glass Secrets

The glossed glares and wide eyes from others
as they looked at me, echoed the ghost of you.

Their eyes showed me who I was before you.
Their eyes showed me who I will be after you.

A shell of a person,
riddled with grief.

A loss so prominent,
it shattered me in two.

Is that all they see when they look at me?

Sea Glass Secrets

I wish time was kind to you.

There is so much I wanted to tell you.
So much I wish I said.

Now I tell it to the stars,
hoping you're there.

Sea Glass Secrets

I've learned something about grief.

If you refuse to acknowledge it, the pain is less searing.
If you refuse to accept it, the loss is less prominent.

Refusal can be a beautiful thing.

It can put a temporary bandage over your heart
to stop the hurt.

It can flood your mind with the memories
you cling desperately to.

It can cast the illusion that hope can
be found even on the darkest of days.

It has been five years now.
I haven't accepted your loss.

The bandage is worn.
The memories are distorted.
The illusion barely illuminates the darkness.

And yet, I still refuse the truth.

Because to acknowledge it is to feel the hurt.

The hurt that forever broke me.

Sea Glass Secrets

Your seat at the dining room table became empty.

It collected dust,
and harboured memories of your laughter.

Your seat in the living room became empty.

It collected dust,
and harboured moments of your scent.

Your seat in the backyard became empty.

It collected dust,
and harboured memories of your favourite songs.

All I have is an empty house.

With dust.
With memories.
With scents.
With songs.

Without you.

Sea Glass Secrets

I haven't seen my mother for three months and counting.
I hear her footsteps and her soft cries at odd hours of the night.
I smell her perfume lingering in the hallway as I walk to my room.

She is becoming one of the ghosts that walk the halls at night.
I know she is there, but I cannot prove it.

I am starting to forget what she looks like.

Anytime I want a reminder,
I look in the mirror.

Sea Glass Secrets

The scars from your loss stretched across our hands.

Hands that were linked together,
yet further apart than ever before.

A family separated by the scars of your loss.

Never to be the same.

Sea Glass Secrets

I used to hate the number 56.

It reminded me of an age you would never reach.

It reminded me of bright lights that robbed you
of the opportunity to do so.

I thought no number could be worse than 56.

Until 57.

Grief is often associated with sadness.
Ululating, sickening sadness.

If they saw the effects of grief on the 57th day.

They would associate it with anger.
They would associate it with violence.
They would associate it with resentment.
They would associate it with irritability.
They would associate it with screaming.
They would associate it with hatred.

Sea Glass Secrets

I resented the world for continuing
to exist without you.

I resented the world for forcing me
to exist without you.

Sea Glass Secrets

The last time I felt sunshine on my face was when you were alive.

It was warm.
It filled me with joy.
It made me loathe rainy days.

Now you are gone, and the sun burns me.

It is cold.
It fills me with sorrow.
It makes me wish for rainy days.

Sea Glass Secrets

Feelings of isolation burrowed
deep into my soul when you died.

I never felt isolated when you were here.
You mended the pain and the sorrow.

You delicately glued parts of my heart that had been
shattered for years, back together again.

Piece by piece.

They no longer hurt me.
They no longer cut me.

I felt whole again.

Until you died, and my heart shattered.

With no one to glue it back together again.

Sea Glass Secrets

The day you died,
my smile eternally dimmed.

I no longer laughed.
I no longer felt joy in the company of others.

I found company in our memories.
I found company in our old photos.

I was breathing.
But I was not living.

I was existing.
It hurts to exist.

Sea Glass Secrets

It held me on my darkest days.
It made uncomfortable social gatherings comfortable.
It numbed the physical pain my heart was subjected to.

With every sip,
I was whisked away from the reality of loss.

The reality of sadness.
The reality of despair.
The reality of grief.

It made my friends think I was fun.
It made me leave the home I knew only as a house.
It made me feel normal.

The fleeting hours where liquid played me like a marionette
allowed me to feel something.

Something other than sadness.
Something other than despair.
Something other than grief.

Sea Glass Secrets

The world stopped turning the day you died.

I felt it.

In my bones.
In my heart.
In every fibre of my being.

I felt it.

The sun stopped being warm.
The night stopped being cool.
The birds no longer sang.

When you died,
the world as I knew it did too.

I did too.

Sea Glass Secrets

The first shooting star I ever saw,
you told me to make a wish.

We linked our hands.
Closed our eyes.

And wished together.

When we opened our eyes,
you told me your wish.

I never told you mine.

The second shooting star I ever saw,
I made a wish.

I linked my hands.
Closed my eyes.

And wished alone.

When I opened my eyes,
I told the darkened sky my wish.

I wished for the stars to return you to me.

Sea Glass Secrets

My worst fear was once
losing you.

My worst fear is now
learning to live in a world without you.

Grief is inescapable.

Sea Glass Secrets

The day you died,
my mother turned into a ghost.

Her howls were heard in the depths of the night.
Her cries were heard in the wake of the morning.
Her absence was felt for weeks at a time.

When you left,
she left too.

Sea Glass Secrets

Memories made by a person whose soul
is no longer with me collect dust in my mind.

They have become distorted.
They have become buried.

They have become forgotten.

I listen to the sound of your voice in a video,
just to remember its tune.

I stare at a picture of you,
just to remember the shape of your smile.

I tell stories of you,
just to remember the way you made me feel.

I listen.
I stare.
I tell.

But I forget.

When the stars took you,
they took my memories too.

Sea Glass Secrets

In another universe,
it would have been me instead of you.

In this universe,
I would have chosen me instead of you.

I wish it was me.

Sea Glass Secrets

I begged the stars for more time with you,
and yet they took you anyway.

They left me guessing where you could have gone.
They left me wondering which star is you.

I wonder why they heard my cries,
and took you anyway.

I wonder why they saw my tears,
and took you anyway.

I wonder why they chose you.

Sea Glass Secrets

I was nine years old
when the stars called you home.

I spent nine years holding your hand.
I spent my tenth year holding grief's hand.

Your loss paved the route of conversations.
Sitting heavy on my shoulders.

When my mother looks at me,
she sees you.

When my siblings look at me,
they see you.

I look like you.
The living and breathing reminder of grief.

Why did the stars need you
more than I did?

I was a child.

Sea Glass Secrets

Your loss burrowed into my spirit.

It carved out the parts of me that felt
each and every human emotion.

Joy.
Love.
Compassion.

It sunk into the parts of me that believed
I would be okay.

Replacing it with sadness.
Replacing it with guilt.
Replacing it with anger.

If I had one more day with you,
I would do everything different.

I would apologize with my heart.
I would appreciate with my heart.
I would love with my heart.

I would savour every moment with you like it was our last.

Knowing it was our last.

Sea Glass Secrets

I'm tired of grieving.

I'm tired of wishing I could sleep my days away,
as that is the only time I see you.

I'm tired of living through photos in my camera roll,
as that is the only time I see you.

I'm tired of grasping at memories,
as that is the only time I see you.

I'm tired of living with grief,
instead of you.

Sea Glass Secrets

The voice of guilt was unkind.

It made me feel remorseful for not
spending my days reciting our last conversation.

It made me feel regretful for not
consuming my nights with memories of you.

It made me feel sorrowful for not
staying in the town where you took your last breath.

The days continued to grow.
The nights continued to grow.
The town continued to grow.

I started to grow.

Grow alongside the grief of losing you,
with the voice of guilt heavy in my ear.

Sea Glass Secrets

I sat in the uncomfortable plastic chair,
watching my classmates cross the stage.

Smiles painted their faces.
Cameras flashing captured the moment.

The sounds of clapping hands echoed in the gymnasium.
The cheers of parents filled the moments of silence.

I once pictured this moment with you.

A smile painted on your face.
A camera flashing capturing my moment.

The sounds of your clapping hands would echo in the gymnasium.
The cheers from your voice would fill the moments of silence.

I am now living this moment without you.

The emptiness I feel mirrors the empty seat beside me.

I hope the stars let you come to earth for a day,
and sit in the empty seat beside me.

Sea Glass Secrets

I will never accept your loss.
I will accept I will be living with it.

Until I take my last breath,
and am reunited with you in the stars.

Until then.

Sea Glass Secrets

Shift

*Sea glass graces the shore, carrying with it secrets
from the waves visible within its transformation.*

Sea Glass Secrets

The waves whispered secrets.
The shores stored answers.

The beach.

The home of many, yet only meaningful to one.

The shifting.

Discarded remnants of once beautiful treasures laid delicately along the shore, a humble gift from the waves to the shifting.

All buried,
except for one.

Its opaque light blue colour washed upon the shore, gracing my toes as it laid in the sand's warmth next to me.

The glass that hurt me.
The glass that I threw into the ocean.

I picked it up and delicately turned it over in my hand,
admiring its grainy texture and smooth edges.

A prism of light, reflecting the early evening sun's glow.
Reflecting beauty for all to see.

I was captivated.

The sea glass rolled in my hand,
before I placed it in my pocket.

I was shifting.

The Shift.

Sea Glass Secrets

My sunshine was stolen from me when I was twelve.

When my siblings looked to me as their parent.
When the loss was too grave to comprehend.
When the nights were too loud, and the days were too silent.
When I was looked at as an outcast yet leaned upon like a pillar.

I searched for my sunshine in every love.
In every therapy session.
In every friendship.
In every connection.

In every place where I believed sunshine to be.

Until I searched within the place I thought it was stolen.

And realized,
the sunshine was me.

Sea Glass Secrets

I searched for a soulmate my entire life.

My soul was bound to my mothers,
and she shattered it with her words.

My soul was bound to my fathers,
and he bruised it with his distance.

My soul was bound to a past lover,
and they damaged it with their deceit.

When the shattering broke my spirit.
When the bruising broke my hope.
When the damage broke my trust.

I picked up a mirror to wipe my tears.

And staring back at me,
was my soulmate.

Sea Glass Secrets

It hurts because it was powerful.
It hurts because it was meaningful.
It hurts because it was purposeful.

Feel every emotion associated with its power.

The euphoria.
The intensity.
The sting.

Feel every emotion associated with its meaning.

The love.
The joy.
The ache.

Feel every emotion associated with its purpose.

The passion.
The light.
The agony.

Feel the hurt to feel the heal.

Sea Glass Secrets

I grew up being told I was not a good person.
You made me believe I was a good person.

I know life hasn't been kind to you.
I am proud of you.

I have trouble fostering true friendships.
You were my first best friend.

Seeing you in pain hurts me more than I let on.
If I could erase your pain, I would.

I tried my hardest to protect you.
I will always keep trying to protect you.

Sea Glass Secrets

You are not what happened to you.
You are so much more than that.

You are a multitude of stories and journeys
that have shaped you to be you.

But they have done just that.
And only that.

Shaped you.
They are not you.

You are more than what happened to you.

Sea Glass Secrets

In the moments where you find your life has been chosen for you,
I hope you find the courage to change it.

I hope you find the heart to leave behind the people who
made you feel small.

I hope you find the strength to abandon a town that
curated your deepest moments of sadness.

I hope you find the voice to express the life you
truly want, rather than be victim to the life that was chosen for you.

I hope you dance effortlessly and love passionately.

With people who make you feel worthy.
In a town that makes you feel joy.
With a voice that makes you feel heard.

Sea Glass Secrets

When the guilt gnaws at you,
it means you are healing.

Healing from the experiences you don't speak about.
Healing from the feelings you don't acknowledge.

The guilt you are feeling are the chains
around your wings becoming loose.

Setting you free.

Free from the experiences that silenced you.
Free from the feelings that you muted.

Try to fly.
I promise you, you can.

Sea Glass Secrets

When I look at you, I see.

I see grief was your only comfort.
I see neglect was your only warmth.
I see pain was your only pleasure.

When I look in the mirror, I no longer see you.

I see me.

I broke the cycle.

Sea Glass Secrets

I thought I was incapable of love.

I never received it.
I never gave it.

I would instead watch it.

Couples strolling through parks.
Whimsical romance on television.
Sunday morning breakfast at diners with passionate conversations.

I thought love to be rare.

It takes a certain type of person to give love.
It takes a certain type of person to receive love.

I was never a certain type of person.

Until you.

I know I am capable of love now.

Sea Glass Secrets

I thought love to be kind.
To be pure.

I thought love was dancing in the rain,
and soft forehead kisses.

But when I found love, I realized it can often not be kind.
It can often not be pure.

It can be passionate conversations,
and moments when you must walk away.

It can be heated arguments,
and moments when you fall into one another.

It can be feelings of suffocation,
and moments when you feel more comfortable being alone.

It can be intrusive thoughts,
and moments of soft reassurance.

Love can be kind.
Love can be pure.

But love can also be a multitude of other things.

I would choose this love over dancing in the rain,
and soft forehead kisses, any day.

I would choose our love over any other love,
any day.

Sea Glass Secrets

I believe that hearts have arms.

A multitude of tiny, microscopic arms that hold you
as you are embraced by another.

The heart's arms not only hold you, but it holds your own heart.

It picks up the pieces.
It smooths the cracks.
It delicately glues it back in place.
It squeezes your heart once to remind it to beat.
It gently releases, leaving you hopeful that it can beat on its own.

That it won't become broken again.

I had searched for the arms from a heart my entire life.

I felt the coldness from my mother's embrace.
I felt the desperation from my siblings' embrace.
I felt the devotion from my father's embrace.

But never the arms.
Until you.

I felt your heart's tiny, microscopic arms hold mine
as you embraced me.

It picked up the pieces.
It smoothed the cracks.
It delicately glued it back in place.
It squeezed my heart once to remind it to beat.

And when you let go of me, it left me feeling hopeful
that my heart can beat on its own.

Sea Glass Secrets

In the time I had known you,
I felt as though I truly knew you.

In the time you had known me,
I felt as though you truly knew me.

You wanted to be loved.
Just how I wanted to be loved.

You wanted to be a kid.
Just how I wanted to be a kid.

As time progressed,
you handed me something.

Something I believed to be lost.

Lost at sea.
Swept under the current from the ocean.

But there it was,
in your hands.

My lifeline.

Sea Glass Secrets

If only you could see yourself from my eyes.

You wouldn't see the darkness.
You wouldn't see the despair.
You wouldn't see the coldness.

That you feel.

You would see the light.
You would see the joy.
You would see the warmth.

That you bring to my life.

Sea Glass Secrets

When you are telling your truth,
do not let anyone minimize it.

Do not let them tell you it is wrong.
Do not let them tell you it did not happen that way.
Do not let them tell you it does not hurt.

If you felt it was right,
don't let them tell you it was wrong.

If you felt it happened a certain way,
don't let them tell you it did not.

If you felt hurt,
don't let them tell you you're not.

What you experienced is your truth.
No one can take that away from you.

Sea Glass Secrets

If I could heal your wounds, I would.
If I could replace your suffering, I would.
If I could bottle up your pain, I would.

Seeing you wounded is the worst pain.
Seeing you suffering is the worst ache.
Seeing you bottle up your pain is the worst sorrow.

I would take it from you any day.

I would care for you how I wished you cared for me.

Sea Glass Secrets

The world needs you.

It needs your kindness.
Your grace.
Your light.

It needs your story.
It needs your lessons.
It needs your journey.

You may not need the world,
but it needs you.

Sea Glass Secrets

My boundaries were always drawn in the sand,
close to the shore.

The waves from the sea would kiss the sand,
and erase the line I drew.

Replacing it with their own line.

A line I tiptoed around.
A line I whispered about.
A line I accepted.

I lived by the sea's line for years.

Tiptoeing around its neglect.
Whispering about its hurt.
Accepting its pain.

Until one day,
I drew my line in the sand again.

Only this time I drew it away from the shore,
and closer to my heart.

Where the sea would never touch it again.

Sea Glass Secrets

The lake where I had my first heartbreak.
The house where I was moulded into a mother.
The steps where my father never stepped.
The hospital where you never returned from.

The town that curated my deepest moments of
sadness grew small in my rear-view mirror.

Leaving behind heartbreak.
Leaving behind neglect.
Leaving behind abandonment.
Leaving behind grief.

Leaving behind my younger self.

Moving towards saving my younger self.

Sea Glass Secrets

Those nights where you held yourself,
someone holds you now.

Those nights where you wished you could escape,
you did.

Those moments where you wanted to feel loved,
you feel it now.

Those hours where you wished the pain away,
it's gone now.

You don't have to keep fighting anymore.
You stopped fighting long ago.

You're okay now.

A letter to my younger self.

Sea Glass Secrets

I knew I was healing when
loud footsteps on stairs no longer made me jump.

I knew I was healing when
crying wasn't only a sign of sadness.

I knew I was healing when
I missed the sun on rainy days.

I knew I was healing when the distance between us grew,
and I didn't feel guilty for letting it.

Sea Glass Secrets

My lungs expanded with oxygen
for the first time in years.

Breathing in oxygen that wasn't plagued
with neglect.

Breathing in oxygen that wasn't plagued
with animosity.

Breathing in oxygen that wasn't plagued
with sorrow.

Breathing in oxygen that wasn't plagued
with heartache.

Is this what being alive feels like?

Sea Glass Secrets

I always believed I was a bad friend.

I couldn't nourish friendships.
I couldn't give my all to others.
I couldn't live up to their expectations.

It ended up in a falling out.

A fight.
A break.

Followed by distance.

Stares.
Glares.

I learned that I didn't need to spend my energy nourishing
friendships that didn't nourish me back.

I learned that I didn't need to give my all to others
that didn't give their all to me back.

I learned that I didn't need to live up to their expectations
when they didn't live up to mine.

I slowly became my own best friend.

It took becoming my own best friend for me to realize that
I *am* a good friend.

It just took the right person to make me believe that.

Sea Glass Secrets

The family that I chose,
chose me back.

It was the first time I had felt chosen.

The first time I had felt seen.
The first time I had felt heard.
The first time I had felt loved.

The feeling of *being* chosen was unfathomable to me.

Being seen.
Being heard.
Being loved.

All unfathomable.

Until them.

They showed me it was fathomable.

Sea Glass Secrets

I grew to know the sound your foot made
on the bottom step of our staircase.

Alerting me to hide.

I grew to know the sound the front door made
when it was about to open.

Alerting me to run.

The stairs became my closest confidant.
The door became my saviour.

My means for survival in a home that felt like a house.

When the sound from the stairs became deafening,
I left.

When the sound from the door became suffocating,
I left.

In the depths of my nightmares, I can still hear the stairs.
I can still hear the door.

In the wake of the morning,
I don't hide.

I don't run.

Sea Glass Secrets

I grew numb to the three-worded phrase *I am sorry.*

It rang in my ears each time it was said.

Its meaning was laced with illusion.
Its intention was paired with empathetic eyes.
Its purpose was matched with disingenuous hugs.

Hugs where I was only there for the purpose of
comforting them about what I endured.

Overtime, I became numb to its worth.

Its meaning.
Its intention.
Its purpose.

Until I heard the phrase *I believe you.*

And the ringing in my ears stopped.

I am sorry made me feel broken beyond repair.
I believe you made me feel understood beyond doubt.

Sea Glass Secrets

I found grief to be lonely.

The ghosts that danced in my darkened bedroom no longer
sufficed as dancing partners.

The lingering feeling of hope that I would one day wake up
and you would be beside me started to consume me.

The sleepless nights where my mind turned to turmoil
replaying every encounter began to distort the memories.

Until it wasn't.

Until I leaned on the girl next door who lost her mother
before she had the chance to become a mother.

Until I spoke with the elderly man at the grocery store who lost
his wife the day before they renewed their vows.

Until I tutored a six-year-old boy who lost his first tooth
the same year he lost his father.

Until I realized that grief didn't make me lonely.

It made me human.

Sea Glass Secrets

I knew I would be okay.

I would be okay because I was whole before you.

I breathed.
I smiled.
I laughed.
I cried.
I felt.

During you, I was still a whole person.

I breathed.
I smiled.
I laughed.
I cried.
I felt.

After you, I was still a whole person.

I just had trouble breathing.
I just had trouble smiling.
I just had trouble laughing.

I cried too hard.
And felt even harder.

But here I am.

Despite it all.
Despite you.

I will be okay.

Sea Glass Secrets

You taught me that loud voices
were heard more than silent ones.

You showed me that neglect
was more compassionate than love.

I grew up silent.
I grew up neglected.

I am now learning to use my voice.
I am now learning to love.

You taught me destruction.
I taught myself restoration.

Sea Glass Secrets

Days after you passed, I was numb.
I believed that if I didn't acknowledge the pain, it wasn't there.

I blinked through the days.
It made it easier to cope.

Months after you passed, I lived every day like you had just died.
I felt every sorrow-filled emotion associated with your passing.

I ached through the days.
It made it easier to cope.

Years after you passed, I went through all five stages of grief.

I felt strong denial in the first year.
I felt ululating anger in the second year.
I felt aching guilt in the third year.
I felt sickening sadness in the fourth year.
I felt a sliver of acceptance in the fifth year.

It has been five years since you've passed.

Each hour feels different.
Each day feels different.
Each month feels different.
Each year feels different.

But that is how I cope.
And that is how I heal.

Sea Glass Secrets

The greatest lesson you ever taught me
was maturity.

You forced me to grow up.
I taught myself to grow.

Sea Glass Secrets

My children will ask about you.

They will ask why your absence fills your seat
at Thanksgiving dinner.

They will ask why your absence shifts the conversation
on Christmas morning.

I will cover the scars latched on my back
from your neglect with a sweater.

I will wipe the tears stained on my face
from your addiction with my hand.

And then I will tell them.

But I won't burden them with historic scars.
But I won't burden them with sorrowful tears.

I will tell them the truth.

The truth that you stopped trying.
The truth that I was tired of trying.

Sea Glass Secrets

I knew you were incapable of giving me the love
I always wished I could receive.

I was reminded with your hands.
I was reminded with your words.
I was reminded with your distance.

The past that branded you like a second skin
was passed down to me like an heirloom.

In the moments where neglect was all you knew,
I gave you my love.

In the moments were coldness replaced your light,
I gave you my warmth.

I forgive you for not knowing how to love me.

I forgive you for me.

Sea Glass Secrets

When you died,
your soul was bound to the stars.

It left me searching for you each night.
It left me guessing which star was you.

I spent years searching the stars.
I spent years guessing where you could have gone.

Until I walked along the beach,
and saw footprints that mirrored yours.

Until I sat on a bench in the park,
and saw your name engraved into it.

Your soul may be in the stars,
yet pieces of you are etched here on earth.

Here with me.

Sea Glass Secrets

When neglect was replaced with love.
When grief was replaced with comfort.
When a house was replaced with a home.

I found the strength to soar.

You made it to the shore.

My final words to you, Sea Glass.

Acknowledgements

To everyone who took a moment to read this book, I cannot thank you enough. My heart feels so full just knowing you read my words. You make me feel heard. You make me feel seen. You make me feel loved.

To my brother, you are my light.

To Andrew and Janet, thank you for your unconditional love. You were both the first people to ever read my original manuscript, and your encouragement, your kindness and your love is what drove me to publish my work. Thank you for being the family I always wanted. There is a poem written in here for you.

To Jacob, thank you for catching my lifeline.

About The Author

Julia Reesor is a Canadian poet and writer who grew up in Ontario, Canada. Her written words began far before she knew what the word "writing" meant and crafted this passion into expressing some of her darkest moments and experiences in the form of poetry and prose.

While her poems capture some of the darkest moments associated with childhood trauma, grief and healing, her stories are close to her heart and for all to read.

After spending the past five years writing her original manuscript, she locked up her work and let them collect dust on her computer. On a whim, she started publishing her work on social media. After finding a community of those who related to her work and resonated with every sorrow-filled emotion packed within her words, she decided to structure a select number of her poems into her first book, *Sea Glass Secrets*.

Julia now lives close to the beach in Ontario, Canada, where she is reminded of the waves that once swallowed her out to sea.

Now, the shore is where she writes.

Sea Glass Secrets

Get in Touch

TikTok: @juliareesorpoetry
Instagram: @juliareesorpoetry
Email: authorjuliareesor@gmail.com